When Is It My TURN?

A Book about Fairness

SANDY DONOVAN

Lerner Publications Company • Minneapolis

Consultant:
Natasha Phillips, MA, Special Education
Special Education Teacher at Beadle
Elementary School
Yankton, South Dakota

Lerner Publications Company
A division of Lerner Publishing Group, Inc.
241 First Avenue North
Minneapolis, MN 55401 U.S.A.

For reading levels and more information, look up this title at
www.lernerbooks.com.

Library of Congress Cataloging-in-Publication Data

Donovan, Sandra, 1967–
     When is it my turn? : a book about fairness / by Sandy Donovan.
        pages   cm. — (Show your character)
     Includes index.
     ISBN 978–1–4677–1364–1 (lib. bdg. : alk. paper)
     ISBN 978–1–4677–2525–5 (eBook)
     1. Fairness—Juvenile literature. I. Title.
   BJ1533.F2D66 2014
   179'.9—dc23   2013022634

Manufactured in the United States of America
1 – MG – 12/31/13

TABLE OF CONTENTS

WITHDRAWN

Sometimes it's easy to know what's fair. It's when everybody shares. Everybody plays by the rules. **And everyone treats everyone else with respect.**

Other times, fairness can be more complicated—like when your dad says you have to make your bed every day, even though your best friend doesn't have to make his! At these times, you have to remember that everyone has different viewpoints. And things in life don't always go exactly as we'd like.

Confused? Read on to sort out what to do when fairness isn't clear-cut. You'll also find **great tips** for keeping things fair in any situation!

In my classroom, there's one comfy reading chair. Everyone fights about who gets to sit there. Today the teacher said that nobody can sit there!

THAT'S NOT FAIR! (IS IT?)

Sometimes things are not how we want them to be. So we say they are not fair. But it's fair when everyone gets a turn.

The kids in your class are fighting. They are not giving everyone a turn. That's not fair. **So maybe it is fair for *nobody* to sit in the chair.**

You can ask your teacher for ideas. What about a sign-up sheet?

Do you have any **other ideas** that might work?

Teachers can be a great resource when you need to talk through tricky problems.

At recess, I want to play four square with my best friends. But other kids always bug us. They want a turn to play too. **CAN'T I JUST PLAY WITH MY FRIENDS?**

It's natural to want to hang out with your friends. But **it's not okay to exclude anyone**.

Also, it's only fair for you to **share**! If you played four square every day with just your friends, you wouldn't be sharing the court with others. Everyone should get a chance to use the court.

Four square is fun to play. Just make sure everyone gets a turn!

But if we let other kids play four square, we're afraid some of them won't follow the rules. Some of the kids in my class even call other kids names at recess. **What should we do if the other kids won't play nicely?**

It's important to follow the rules. That's part of being fair. **And it's never okay to call anyone a name.**

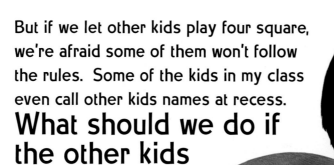

If kids won't play fair, you can ask them not to play. If they call you names, ask them to stop. If they won't stop, **tell an adult**.

Be respectful, and ask others to be respectful. If they won't, talk to an adult.

In our class, our teacher picks one person every week to be class leader. Everyone gets to be the leader at least once. But it seems like some kids don't care if they get to lead or not.

WHY DOES EVERYONE NEED TO HAVE A TURN?

It's important to give everyone a chance.

Some people may say they don't want a turn. But really, they might be disappointed if they never got to lead. Others might feel nervous about speaking up and asking for a turn. They should get a turn. **It's the fair thing to do.**

Including everyone is the thoughtful thing to do.

I lost my favorite pen. A kid named Ben found it. He said he's keeping it. He thinks that's fair. But I don't think it is. It's still my pen.

WHAT IF WE CAN'T AGREE ON WHAT'S FAIR?

The fair thing to do is **talk about it**. Tell Ben what you think is fair. And listen to what he thinks is fair. Listening is an important part of being fair.

If you still don't agree, **ask an adult** what he or she thinks is fair.

Sometimes it is difficult to work out what is fair. In these cases, you may want to involve an adult.

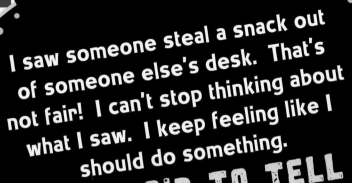

I saw someone steal a snack out of someone else's desk. That's not fair! I can't stop thinking about what I saw. I keep feeling like I should do something. **IS IT FAIR TO TELL ON SOMEONE?**

Telling on a classmate can be uncomfortable. But if someone does something *really* wrong—like stealing or picking on someone else—it's what you need to do.

You know you don't feel right about seeing someone steal. And whenever you have a bad feeling that just won't go away, it's a sign that you should act. You should **speak up** about what you saw.

Telling on a classmate can be hard, but sometimes it is necessary.

You may worry that the person who stole will know you're the one who told. But you can tell your teacher in private. Then you can let your teacher decide how to handle it. You'll feel better knowing that you **took action** rather than ignoring your feelings.

It's not fair for adults to take advantage of others. And cutting in line is taking advantage of other people's time. It can be a good idea to tell if you see something unfair. You should always tell if someone's getting hurt. But sometimes, the **polite thing** to do is to not say anything at all.

Why should you speak up at some times and not at others? Well, nothing terrible will happen if someone cuts in line. Besides, like it or not, kids need to **show respect** to adults. And showing respect sometimes means minding your own business—unless someone's actions are really harming someone else. That's why your mom asked you not to say anything.

21

I got in trouble for kicking my sister underneath the kitchen table. But she kicked me first!

WHY DID I GET IN TROUBLE WHEN IT'S SOMEONE ELSE'S FAULT?

Your sister may have kicked first. But you had a choice about kicking her back. **You can control your own actions.**

22

It's not fair to blame your sister for the way that you reacted. Your parents want to make sure you know that. The next time your sister acts up, remember not to respond to bad behavior with bad behavior of your own.

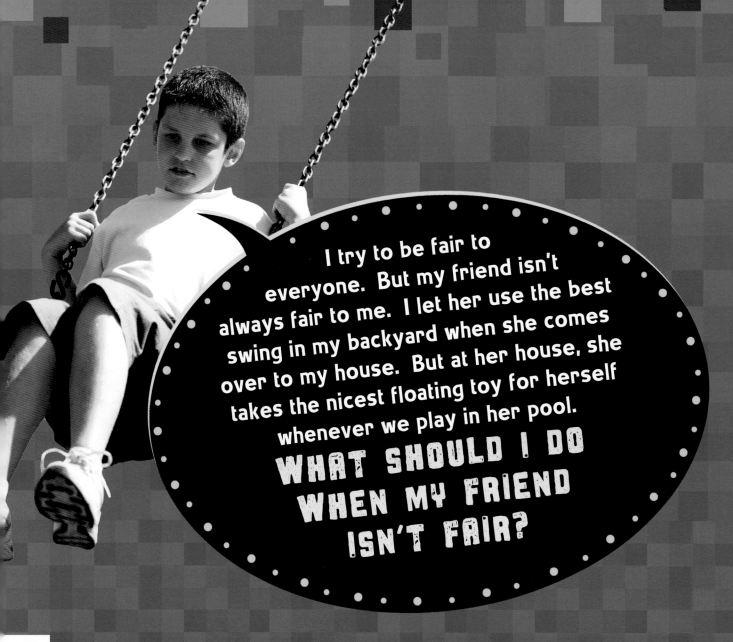

I try to be fair to everyone. But my friend isn't always fair to me. I let her use the best swing in my backyard when she comes over to my house. But at her house, she takes the nicest floating toy for herself whenever we play in her pool.

WHAT SHOULD I DO WHEN MY FRIEND ISN'T FAIR?

First, talk to your friend. Explain how it makes you feel when you don't get a turn to use the floating toy. **Listen** to what she has to say. Maybe she didn't even realize you wanted to use the toy!

When you talk it out and find fair ways to share, you and your friends can all have fun!

If your friend doesn't seem to get where you're coming from, maybe the two of you just have different ideas about what's fair. Then you need to work something out that you can both agree to. Ask if she'd mind letting you use the toy every other time you play in the pool. Or maybe you can claim the best swing when you play at your house, and she can take the best floating toy when you play at hers. Whatever you agree to, it needs to feel fair to both of you.

Parents often set rules about the foods kids eat, when they go to bed, and how much TV they watch. They make these rules to try to keep you healthy.

Adults can be fair the same way kids can. They can share things with you. They can give you turns. They can listen to what you have to say. They can respect you. But they can still set the rules. That's fair!

QUIZ: FAIR OR UNFAIR?

Now it's your turn to judge what's fair or not! Read through the five examples below, and decide which are fair and which are unfair. When you're done with the quiz, check your answers against the key at the bottom of the next page.

- At a birthday party, you really wanted a piece of cake with flowers on top, but the girl in front of you got the last one. Fair or unfair?

- You told your dad that you saw your sister eating a piece of candy before dinner, but all your dad did was tell you not to tattle. And your sister didn't even get in trouble! Fair or unfair?

- You really wanted to be first in line at lunchtime, but the lunch monitor said it was someone else's turn. Fair or unfair?

- You called your classmate a name because he called you a name first, and now your teacher is punishing *you*! You have to stay in at recess. Fair or unfair?

- You told your mom three good reasons why you should be allowed to stay up late, but she still made you go to bed. Fair or unfair?

Key: The truth is that all of these examples are fair!
Did you guess correctly?

complicated: something that has many parts and can be hard to understand

exclude: to leave somebody out

respect: consideration or courtesy. If you treat someone with respect, you treat him or her how you would like to be treated.

take advantage: to do something just for the purpose of helping yourself—even if it hurts someone else

viewpoint: the way that someone sees a particular situation

FURTHER INFORMATION

"Cheating"
http://kidshealth.org/kid/feeling/school/cheating.html
Is it ever fair to cheat? Read this interesting article and find out.

Crist, James J., and Elizabeth Verdick. *Siblings: You're Stuck with Each Other, So Stick Together.* Minneapolis: Free Spirit Publishing, 2010. Read this book for some good advice about how to figure out what's fair and what's not between brothers and sisters.

Donovan, Sandy. *How Can I Deal with Bullying? A Book about Respect.* Minneapolis: Lerner Publications, 2014. Learn more about respect, and find out how to handle tricky situations involving bullying.

"How to Be a Good Sport"
http://kidshealth.org/kid/feeling/emotion/good_sport.html
Check out this article to find tips about how to lose gracefully. You'll also find information on how to be a good sport.

Rosenthal, Amy Krouse. *It's Not Fair!* New York: HarperCollins, 2008. This hilarious illustrated book will make you think twice the next time you feel like shouting out, "It's not fair!"

INDEX

PHOTO ACKNOWLEDGMENTS

The images in this book are used with the permission of: © Purestock/Thinkstock, p. 4; © Digital Vision/ Thinkstock, pp. 5, 13; © Stock4B/Getty Images, p. 6; © Fuse/Getty Images, p. 7; © Gideon Mendel/ Corbis, pp. 8, 17; © Scholastic Studio 10/Getty Images, p. 9; © Kevin Cozad/O'Brien Productions/ CORBIS, p. 11; © Nancy R. Cohen/Photodisc/Getty Images, p. 12; © Klaus Vedfelt/Riser/Getty Images, p. 14; © iStockphoto.com/Squaredpixels, p. 15; © Kevin Dodge/ Radius Images/Getty Images, pp. 18, 19; © iStockphoto.com/bowdenimages, p. 20; © Mark Bowden/E+/Getty Images, p. 23; © Alix Minde/PhotoAlto/ Getty Images, pp. 24, 25; © B. Pepone/Corbis, p. 26; © Jack Hollingsworth/Photodisc/Thinkstock, p. 27.

Front Cover: © Kwame Zikomo/SuperStock.

Main body text set in ChurchwardSamoa Regular. Typeface provided by Chank.